IT'S ABOUT TIME

Time Management For Church Professionals

R. Franklin Gillis, Jr.

C.S.S. Publishing Co.
Lima, Ohio

IT'S ABOUT TIME

BV
4379.5
.G55
1989

Second Printing 1989

9827 / ISBN 1-55673-116-7   PRINTED IN U.S.A.

Contents

Preface and Acknowledgements

The practice of effective time use continues to be a major concern for church professionals. This book is a tool which can give practical assistance for more productive time use. It is the result of experience, practice and learnings from participating in and leading time-management seminars.

I am grateful to many persons who have made contributions which have resulted in this book: to Dr. James D. Glasse, who first taught me the meaning of "time management," and to colleagues who have participated with me in time-management workshops and encouraged me in this work. Special thanks are extended to Maynard Hatcher, a gifted author and valued friend, for his suggestions. I am particularly grateful to my wife, Betty, for all the time she invested in this project. It is to her and others who sense the value of time as God's gift to be used to the fullest that I dedicate this work.

R. Franklin Gillis, Jr.
Portsmouth, Virginia

Introduction

Time is our most precious possession. Time provides an opportunity to be with people, to perform tasks, or to do nothing. What we do with our time is what we do with our lives. In order to have full lives, we must make the best use of time. We do not have to keep busy every minute of every day but we should spend our precious time on what is important personally and professionally. Our lives are measured in terms of time. The more we manage our time use, the more we are managing life.

I am a church professional who, in order to fulfil my ministry, has learned that I must be a time-management practitioner. What is shared here is the result of the last eight years' practice of becoming a better time user. These principles are based upon the learnings of twenty-three years in professional church ministry. Behind these principles lies the conviction that time is a gift from God and that we are called to be faithful stewards of our time.

This book is brief because time is important. It is a summary of the most important issues involved in the practice of effective use of time. My goal is to provide the reader with information and exercises resulting in more effective time use.

— R. Franklin Gillis

Part I

Answering Some Questions About Time Use

Chapter One

Do You Have the Time?

How often have you heard someone say, "I wish I had more time"; "I just don't have time"; or "Some day, when I have more time . . ."? These are familiar thoughts and expressions for all of us. "Once upon a time," I thought the same way.

Many people keep wishing for more time because they are convinced they don't have enough time to do what they need or want to do.

The truth is, we all have the same amount of time. Time is measured by twenty-four hours each day, seven days a week, and three hundred sixty-five days a year. Someone has even used time to calculate that there are eight-thousand, seven-hundred-sixty hours in a year. That's a lot of time when viewed collectively. So what's the problem? Why do we wish we "had more time"? What are we really saying? The answers to these questions have to do with time management.

As church professionals, many demands are placed upon our time. Ministry is a multifaceted profession filled with regular duties and responsibilities, immediate needs and long-term projects, long hours, evening meetings, unexpected interruptions, emergencies, and the pressure of deadlines. How does one survive the ministry when there isn't enough time to do everything?

The answer is more effective use of the time given us. To be most productive in ministry, church professionals must develop and practice time-management techniques. Because of the nature of church work, we have to work hard at effective time use. Professional church workers do not quit in the middle of a meeting or while working on a project "because it's quitting time" according to the clock. Clocks aren't the motivators for church professionals the way they are for many in the secular world.

Perhaps you have worked in an environment where a whistle blew at a certain hour to mark the beginning of the work day. If so, you can identify with Bill.

"That stupid whistle! I get so tired of hearing that whining noise."

"Boy, Bill, you're grouchy this morning. Get up on the wrong side of the bed?"

"Naw. I'm just tired of living by a whistle. Whistle to go to work. Whistle to eat lunch. Whistle to get back to work."

"But don't forget the biggie."

"Yeah, I know. The whistle to go home. But then it just starts all over again."

"Tough, buddy. But, that one was to go to work so we'd better get at it."

Perhaps you have had such a regimented life. I have, and I felt just like Bill. During that period of my life I did not have much appreciation for time. It was too precisely measured by whistles and watching the clock. I was too young to value time so I wished it away, eager for weekend free time.

After several years of working a forty-hour week for my employer, I decided to prepare for ordained Christian ministry. As a minister I sought to be a faithful steward by seeing how many hours I could work in a day and how many nights I could fill with commitments. Somehow, I lost control of my time. My denominational "little black book" (pocket appointment calendar) was always available whenever I was asked to take on a task. I carried it everywhere because it was a status symbol which helped define who I was. A problem arose. I became a slave to my appointment book and practiced "time abuse."

Time cures many things, and I grew a little wiser. The actual turning point came from participating in a time-management seminar at Lancaster Theological Seminary.

We got up at the crack of dawn. Two colleagues joined me for the day-long seminar and we had to get an early start for the three-hour drive. On the way we wondered what awaited us.

"This had better be good," voiced one of my colleagues, bemoaning the fact that he would be a day behind in his work because of going.

"Maybe he'll show us how to find more hours in the day," replied the other.

I couldn't help but identify with both statements. I, too, was leaving unfinished work behind. But the subject of the seminar intrigued me. I needed whatever this opportunity offered and I prayed that the time spent would be beneficial.

Time passed quickly as we talked our way to Lancaster, Pennsylvania. Dr. James Glasse began the seminar on time. His subject was time, but it was time in dimensions and relationships based upon individual time use that proved revealing.

When it was over, my colleagues and I agreed that the event was one of the best uses of time ever spent in a seminar. We came away with a new appreciation for time and a new commitment to making time work more productively in ministry.

Reflecting on the experience points to an important truth: *the time which we control is the most valuable time of all*. This has become more important now that I am a church professional and have basic control over my schedule. Much of what I share in the present volume is a direct result of that learning event — and the trying and testing of time-management principles over the last eight years.

It is easy to get bogged down and give all of our time to one aspect of ministry at the expense of some other equally important responsibility. We get sidetracked from the things we intend to do and need to do. Because we don't punch a time clock, or account for our time to another person, or aren't engaged in tasks with easily defined beginnings and endings, we become frustrated about our poor management of time. If that's where you are, there is good news! That can all be changed. We can become more productive, get lots more done in less time, and still have time for ourselves.

Sound too good to be true? Spend a few minutes now with this exercise and you will be on the way to more effective time use.

Your Time-Management Rating

Below are ten questions which will help you determine how you manage your time. Put a check mark after each question in the appropriate column. Use the number at the top of each column for scoring. Compare your total of all questions with the rating scale below.

	Often 5 points	Sometimes 3 points	Seldom 1 point	Never 0 points
1. Do you take on more than one major task at a time?	☐	☐	☐	☐
2. Do you worry about work or take work home with you?	☐	☐	☐	☐
3. Do you have trouble remembering if you have done something?	☐	☐	☐	☐
4. Do interruptions interfere with your work?	☐	☐	☐	☐
5. Are there times when you are uncertain about what to do next?	☐	☐	☐	☐
6. Do you spend considerable time on details?	☐	☐	☐	☐
7. Do you fail to delegate tasks which could lighten your work load?	☐	☐	☐	☐
8. Do you keep your desk and work area neat and organized?	☐	☐	☐	☐
9. Are your files and records organized and up to date?	☐	☐	☐	☐
10. Do you worry about what you didn't accomplish when the day is over?	☐	☐	☐	☐
Total	___ +	___ +	___ +	___ =

My total _____

Time-Management Rating Scale:

35-50 — You manage your time poorly. You need to read this book carefully and possibly consider taking a time-management course.

16-34 — You are average in your time management but there are areas where you can improve.

0-15 — Congratulations. You manage your time well. If you scored 0-5, and you were honest with your answers, you don't need this book. Give it to a friend!

Exercise 1

Chapter Two

Where Does the Time Go?

Eddie was about to celebrate his fortieth birthday. He was not looking forward to it. His life had been so consumed with church work that he had hardly taken time for celebrations of any kind. He wondered where the years had gone. He also wondered how many more years he could give to the demands of the ministry. Eddie was experiencing burn-out and he needed help. A colleague, sensing Eddie's problem, suggested that he see a counselor. Reluctantly he went.

After several sessions, Eddie's counselor handed him a sheaf of papers. He examined them casually.

"What are these?" he asked.

"Time logs," the counselor replied. "They are fairly self-explanatory. I want you to post them in detail," he smiled, "religiously."

"I know what I do with my time," Eddie snapped, laying the papers on the desk.

"I suggest that you do not." He handed them back to Eddie. "This is not a request. This is a prescription that you must fill if we are to reach our goal."

Eddie folded the sheaf, and tucked it in his inside coat pocket. "What goal?" he asked.

"Regaining control of your life."

Good time management involves the best use of time to accomplish life's professional and personal goals. It also involves what we do with time, not how much time we have. The term "time management" is actually a misnomer. Actual management of time is beyond our control. What is implied by the term is management of ourselves with respect to time. We need to think of it as a process of controlling events. Efficiency is not getting more done in less time. Time management is arranging to accomplish the things we choose to get done within the time available.

Effective users of time must go through a learning process of evaluating time use and behavior modification. To become effective users of time we begin by examining our time use, not with examining tasks to do nor with planning how to do the tasks. Time-management experts suggest that more effective time use begins by determining how we actually use time. Therefore, we start by finding out where our time actually goes.

Time management is similar to the management of money. Those who effectively manage their financial affairs operate on a budget and a careful analysis of how money is spent based upon desired goals. If money runs out at the end of the month, we must analyze our use of money to determine the problem, and select appropriate corrective actions. Time can be managed the same way.

If we want to gain better control over our time, we must analyze the past before looking to the future. This is best done by using a time log. A time log is a written record of what happens (or, perhaps more accurately, *what we choose to do*) in a given period of time. Time logs are important for a number of reasons. Unless we keep a log, we tend to inaccurately account for our time. We might imagine a given project taking several hours when actually it took only one hour and the remaining time was taken by interruptions. Completing time logs enables us to see what priorities we have in our lives based upon the amount of time given each event. Time logs also help us pinpoint what happens so that we might make appropriate changes leading to more effective time use. By recording time use, we begin to change our behavior with regard to time. Most time-management consultants recommend that time logs be kept for several weeks consecutively. This provides sufficient data for analysis.

The process which leads to more effective time use begins with five initial steps:

First, *record* how time is spent. (Two time logs are provided at the end of this chapter.) Write down everything done in given time periods. Include personal time as well as professional time.

Second, *analyze* the time log. Analysis will make obvious what tasks take most time. Examine present time use against the background of questions included in the exercise at the end of this chapter.

Third, *evaluate* how time is spent against the goals and objectives. Periodically establishing goals and objectives is important in providing direction for ministry.

Fourth, *experiment* with including new patterns of doing things, and shifting of priorities. For example, after analyzing the time log, complete this sentence: "I'm going to find more time for . . ." Then find time to do it.

Finally, *repeat* this process periodically. Completing time logs (perhaps every three to six months) will facilitate striving toward better control and will develop better and more productive time-use principles.

You will soon be able to determine how to improve time use by analyzing and deciding between unimportant and important tasks.

Analyzing time use should reveal many obstacles in

developing more effective time use. There are many "time robbers" which prohibit this. "Time robbers" are things which keep us from doing other things which have more value or importance to us. We will be identifying specific "time robbers" in chapter eight.

In the meantime, as we begin to gain a new sense of how we spend time, be on the lookout for those low-value activities which tend to get in the way of productive time use. Effective time use is an art toward which we should strive as we seek to be faithful stewards of the gift of time.

Time Logs

Two time logs are provided to record time use. Be as thorough as possible with this exercise. When you have completed time logs for at least two weeks, ask yourself the following questions:

- To what tasks did I give too little time?

- To what tasks did I give too much time?

- With what tasks did I procrastinate?

- What were my priorities based on amount of time committed?

- What changes should I implement in my use of time?

Exercise 2

Time Log   **Week One**

	MON	TUE	WED
7:00 am			
8:00			
9:00			
10:00			
11:00			
Noon			
1:00 pm			
2:00			
3:00			
4:00			
5:00			
6:00			
7:00			
8:00			
9:00			
10:00			
11:00			

Time Log   Week One

THUR	FRI	SAT	SUN

Time Log   Week Two

	MON	TUE	WED
7:00 am			
8:00			
9:00			
10:00			
11:00			
Noon			
1:00 pm			
2:00			
3:00			
4:00			
5:00			
6:00			
7:00			
8:00			
9:00			
10:00			
11:00			

Time Log   Week Two

THUR	FRI	SAT	SUN

Chapter Three

Why Do You Do What You Do?

Once upon a time there was a minister who thought he could do and be all things to all people. The key to effective ministry, he was sure, was to keep busy, rush from one thing to the next, and never waste time. He was convinced that successful ministry was based upon keeping an appointment book filled with meetings, activities, and appointments. In fact, to assure that an opportunity was never missed, he always kept his appointment book with him and was quick to make commitments on the spot.

Of course, a "guardian angel" would protect him from all harm and illnesses (such as ulcers, mental and physical exhaustion or heart attack) and some day his efforts would be rewarded by assignment to the perfect multi-staffed church where he would live happily ever after. Or, if not that, perhaps a church would recognize the sincere dedication indicated by his busy schedule, and he would earn a high administrative position. He was sure that there would be "pie in the sky by and by" if only he worked hard enough.

Such a scenario is not unheard of in this day and time, but persons who drive themselves this way often end up having heart attacks and other health problems.

Time is life. To waste time is to waste life. In time management, questions about what we do with our time are actually inquiries about what we are doing with life. Each person decides daily how to use their time allocation to achieve whatever he or she determines to be important toward the fulfilment of individual life goals. Time management is a matter of prioritizing life values and arranging time use to facilitate them. Effective time management, therefore, is a uniquely personal experience of determining life goals, becoming aware of behavioral patterns, and using time to fulfil goals in the most efficient way.

Why *do* you do what you do? Most church professionals would answer that question by saying, "It's my job." The conflict comes when the demands placed upon "my job" exceed "the time," and that happens every day! Who determines what your job involves? What are your roles as a church professional? Do you seek to fulfil a predetermined job description or are you expected to figure out your ministry by yourself?

I have found it helpful to work with my Staff-Parish Committee in determining time use based on priorities for ministry. Some of the roles I assume because of who I am never change, but there are shifts in the roles according to seasons of the year. For example, fall is a heavy administrative time in my denomination. By communicating with the committee about the requirements for this time of year, I am allowed to relinquish other responsibilities in order to accomplish the necessary annual administrative tasks. The committee also helps interpret (and defend when necessary) my time use to the total congregation so that I will not be expected to fulfil all the expectations of the members.

A sample "responsibility list" is included at the end of this chapter, along with an exercise sheet, so that you may develop your own list based upon your understanding of your work. Of course your list will also be determined by your understanding of your specific responsibilities (required by job title) as well as special talents and skills which you bring to your ministry. Encourage the committee in your church to whom you have primary accountability to assist you in determining priorities for ministry as they perceive them. Then you will be able to determine your priorities based on the church's priority expectations and to reconcile the differences. This can be done creatively when honest and open communication occurs.

Life is composed of three categories of responsibilities: the *"have to's,"* the *"ought to's"* and the *"want to's."* There are a certain number of "have to's" that go with every profession. Those are the unavoidable tasks which must be done for the job.

There are the "want to's," which make the job worthwhile. Those are the tasks which are enjoyable, delightful, and if we could choose, we would spend all our time doing what we "want to" do, for this brings about the greatest sense of personal satisfaction.

Then, there are the "ought to's" which tend to bog us down. How many times have you said this past week, "I know I ought to . . ."? The "ought to's" are not great motivators for ministry. In fact, they are often responsible for procrastination. A secret of successful ministry is to eliminate as many of the "ought to's" as possible so that we might spend more productive time on the "want to's" and the "have to's."

It would be helpful for you to identify the various tasks you performed in ministry this past week and categorize them. (See Exercise 4) Ask this question concerning the "ought to's" that you felt compelled to do: "What would happen if I didn't . . . (hadn't. . .)?"

Someone has suggested "the problem with ministry is that often we feel we ought to do what we have to do when we don't want to." Most productive ministry comes when we spend the largest portion of time with the "want to's," a moderate amount of time with the "have to's," and a minimal amount of time with the "ought to's," working to get rid of this latter category altogether.

Time logs (discussed in the previous chapter) allow you to see how many hours you work in a given week.

Do you work more then sixty hours a week? Do you have difficulty taking a regular day off?

While random stories of unconscionable laziness crop up, one of the typical pitfalls of church professionals is a compulsiveness to be doing something all the time, since there is always more to be done. There are a number of reasons for compulsiveness. Some people are compulsive workers because they're trying to prove their worth. For others, compulsiveness is brought on by a fear of failure.

It is easy for church professionals to become compulsive because it is difficult to measure results or accomplishments. Feedback is often difficult to obtain when we are doing well. We normally hear only when dissatisfactions occur. So, to convince ourselves that we are doing a good job, we work long and hard. If you tend to fall into the category of a compulsive church professional, begin now to ask, "Why do I do what I do?"

All demands upon your time must be measured against your own understanding of your talents, skills, gifts and commitments to ministry. Say *no* to the demands that don't fit your role. You need to say no often because church professionals today, especially clergy, are asked to play many other roles, and some are not a legitimate use of the church professional's time. Watch out for the "ought to's." Life is too short to be spending time unwisely and non-productively as Christ's servants!

My Responsibilities in Ministry

1. List ten of the most important things you do as a church professional:

___ 1. _____

___ 2. _____

___ 3. _____

___ 4. _____

___ 5. _____

___ 6. _____

___ 7. _____

___ 8. _____

___ 9. _____

___ 10. _____

2. Using the spaces provided at the left, prioritize your list according to importance in your ministry (1 as the most important and 10 as the least important task).

3. Have a friend or church member who knows you well make a list of ten of the most important things he or she thinks you do as a church professional. Ask that the list be prioritized. Compare your friend's list with your list. What have you learned from this exercise about how you are presently using your time?

Exercise 3

Tasks Performed in Ministry

Review your activities of last week and identify them according to the following motivations:

"Have to's"   **"Want to's"**   **"Ought to's"**

Analyze your list. What "ought to's" could have been eliminated? Did you spend more time doing "have to's," "want to's" or "ought to's"? What adjustments can you make to future time use based on these findings?

Exercise 4

Responsibilities in Ministry

Note: The following list is an example of one that may be used with a staff parish relations or personnel committee to assist the church professional in determining priorities for tasks of ministry. This list represents primary tasks of a pastor and is provided only as a model. Each church professional should develop his/her own list which represents the position's job description, and the talents and skills which she or he brings to the position. Such a list should be reviewed with the committee periodically so that together they may dialogue concerning effective time use in addressing the church's ministry. The instructions will guide the committee in the completion of such a *Responsibilities in Ministry* form.

Instructions:

Begin by discarding three tasks of ministry. (This is done as a reminder that the staff member cannot do or be all things.) Then prioritize the remaining tasks by beginning with the number 1 as the most important. Make your decisions based on your knowledge of the church's needs and the pastor's skills.

_____ Attending meetings

_____ Sermon preparation

_____ Hospital visitation

_____ Visiting inactive members

_____ Visiting and cultivating new members

_____ Visiting shut-ins

_____ Worship planning

_____ Administration

_____ Teaching

_____ Counseling

_____ Denominational responsibilities beyond the local church

_____ Community and civic responsibilities

_____ Staff meetings/planning

_____ Assisting the needy

_____ Continuing education and personal growth

_____ Providing leadership training for church officers

_____ Public relations

_____ Other _____

Chapter Four

Are Meetings Worth the Time?

Seven of the nine members of the committee gathered for the meeting and engaged in casual conversation. The appointed hour to begin had passed.

"I wonder where Bob and Sue are," the chairperson said. "I know it's time to start, but since they aren't here, let's give them a few more minutes."

The committee members returned to their informal conversation. Several looked at their watches. One appeared annoyed by the delay.

Fifteen minutes after the appointed hour the chairperson finally said, "Well, I guess we had better get started. Maybe Bob and Sue will come. I hope they know we are meeting. Will the monthly meeting of the committee come to order? Now, does anyone remember what we did when we last met? Or better yet, does anyone know what we need to do tonight?"

Some laughter followed. Two hours later, no one was laughing. Most were tired, frustrated and discouraged from the lack of accomplishment.

What could a church professional do to correct the common mistakes represented in such a meeting?

Church professionals invest many hours a week in meetings. Meetings go with the profession and there isn't much we can do about it.

Many church meetings are unnecessary. Of those that fill a need, many are poorly planned and managed. Frequently, meetings do not begin on time with no set ending time established. Such meetings are great time-wasters.

Time-management principles will increase the

quality and decrease the quantity of meetings. Let's consider several recommendations for more productive meeting time. The first is a simple rule: don't hold meetings that aren't necessary. Many churches have regularly-scheduled meetings on the second Tuesday (or you name the day) of the month, and that meeting is held, no matter what!

As that time draws near, the chairperson, or the staff person relating to that committee, assumes responsibility to see that the meeting takes place. But what about the purpose of the meeting? Has an agenda been planned in advance? Are there specific actions which must occur? Are there specific decisions to be made? If not, consider whether the meeting needs to be held.

It is also worth considering alternative ways to reach decisions. In some cases, phone conversations with committee members will serve the purpose and save considerable time.

We fail to take into account the tremendous resource that every church meeting represents. For example, if a committee meeting has eight members attending, this represents an expenditure (in total time) of two work days, or sixteen hours' investment. Meetings should be held only if they are the best way to make decisions and represent the maximum utilization of the participants' time. (See Exercise 5 for meeting evaluation.)

Effective meetings begin in advance by defining the objective, and should be planned with two key questions in mind: "Why are we here?" and "What do we want to accomplish?" For meetings in which vital decisions will be made, it is important to plan and distribute an advance agenda. This encourages prior consideration and preparation by committee members. Time is saved when members have done their thinking in advance of the meeting and come ready to express their opinions. A prepared agenda with notations of each item keeps the meeting moving. Such notations as "For information," "For discussion," "For decision," enable the participants to know what is expected of each item on the agenda.

Effective meetings are run by effective leaders who value time and who make the most of that given by others. A skillful leader holds the participants to the agenda and provides the momentum to keep the meeting moving toward the desired goals within the allocated time frame.

Incidentally, effective leaders of meetings never ask the fatal question, "Is there anything more we need to discuss?" Discussion items were determined when the agenda was formulated and such a question is an invitation to waste time. If an item is not on the agenda, it doesn't need to be discussed. A suggested agenda for church meetings is included at the end of this chapter (Exercise 6).

Meetings should also begin and adjourn on time. Announcing the starting time and the adjourning time keeps the meeting moving and reduces frustration because of unrealized expectations. Every meeting needs a time limit. The leader should commit publicly to the time the meeting will end and stick to the time commitment, or end earlier if the work has been accomplished. (I have never known those in attendance to be upset by a meeting that ended *before* the announced time!)

Experience indicates that most meetings need no more than one hour and that the most productive meetings are held within that time frame. Parkinson's law applies here: "The task assigned fills the time allotted." It's amazing how much work a committee actually does in the last ten minutes prior to adjournment *when the adjournment time is known.* No one wants to go overtime, for we are conditioned to spend time in segments, and when that time has been used, we are ready and eager to move on to the next thing on our personal agendas. A limit set ahead of time has a psychological effect upon the meeting participants. Limits also tend to cut out nonessential conversation and less important items will be left out until they become important.

Ideally, each meeting should have a written record of business transacted and it should be duplicated and distributed to all members prior to the next meeting. The "minutes" (along with the agenda) will remind members of the tasks to be completed in the upcoming meeting. Minutes received by members who were absent from the previous meeting also serve to help bring the absent members up-to-date concerning the committee's work. Properly-written minutes include a list of persons present, a summary of each item discussed, and a brief description of actions and/or decisions. Including a listing of absent members might prompt their subsequent attendance.

Church professionals do not have to, nor should they, attend all church meetings. In fact, there are some meetings that would probably go better without the presence of the professional, for such presence often hampers leaders in exercising their talents and responsibilities.

An effective model involves holding necessary committee meetings on the same night at the same time. The church professional's primary role is to be a resource person available to the committee upon request. Sometimes I spend the whole time allotment with one committee if their agenda warrants my presence. Other times I spend portions of time in several settings, mostly listening and being available as needed.

If you are in a position to call meetings, ask yourself some basic questions: Is this meeting necessary? What actions should result from the proposed meeting? What is my role?

If you have responsibility for seeing that others hold meetings, you can enable effective meetings. Help the person in charge of the meeting raise the above questions.

The most important thing is to move meetings toward actions, decisions, and assignments. Many meetings end with participants unsure of what was decided, what is supposed to happen next, and by whom. People become more willing to attend committee meetings if significant work is involved. Church professionals have the responsibility of ensuring that meetings have value and that they are a vital part of developing ministry.

Let me add a suggestion to insure that meeting times will be productive. Carry a notepad and pencil to all meetings. If the meeting requires only your presence and not involvement, spend your time productively on other tasks. I find this is a tremendous time saver! Such action isn't discourteous; it's good time use. Besides, no one will know that you're not taking notes of the meeting!

Meeting Evaluation

Review the last church meeting you attended and answer yes or no to the following statements in the space provided for each.

	YES	NO
1. The meeting needed to take place	☐	☐
2. The purpose of the meeting was clear	☐	☐
3. There was a prepared agenda	☐	☐
4. We kept only to items on the agenda	☐	☐
5. The chairperson had good control	☐	☐
6. Important decisions were made	☐	☐
7. My contribution was crucial to the outcome	☐	☐
8. The amount of time spent was appropriate	☐	☐
9. The meeting began and ended on time	☐	☐
10. I needed to be there the whole time	☐	☐

Based on your reponse to the above statements, what specific recommendations can you make for future meetings?

Exercise 5

Suggested Agenda for Church Meetings

Meeting of _____

Date _____ Time frame _____

Agenda review and adoption (Chairperson's name _____)

Additional agenda items
●
●

Prayer for our work (name _____)

Attendance record and minutes from last meeting

Reports (and by whom)
●
●
●

Actions Required/Decisions pending
●
●

Calendar review (deadlines, upcoming events, next meeting, etc.)
●
●

Adjournment with blessing by (name _____)

Exercise 6

Chapter Five

Are You Organized for Ministry?

To become organized for ministry we do well to practice the principle expressed in the rule, "a place for everything and everything in its place!" Being organized for ministry has to do with organizing time and being able to find what is needed when you need it. We have addressed the organization of time use based on priorities for ministry. Now let's address the organization of resources through systems.

Organization for ministry begins in the office. For example, you receive a phone call from a member who wants to know the specifics concerning actions taken at a committee meeting several weeks ago. How long would it take you to find a copy of the minutes or your notes from that meeting so you could answer the question? If you said, "thirty seconds or less," you already have an organizational system that works for you. But if your answer was, "I'll have to get back with you on that," because you couldn't readily put your hands on the necessary information, then you need to work on organization.

Church professionals need to be good administrators with effective organizational skills. These characteristics may not come naturally or easily. Becoming an effective administrator involves willingness to accept the administrative role as a legitimate part of ministry and to acquire the necessary skills. To validate that role for ministry, I have developed a system that supports my work. I have become a form-and-file person through the realization that forms and files are vital, due to the diverse nature of ministry. Whatever else I may be as a church professional, I am a resource person and am expected to have information concerning the church's ministry. Therefore, my system of organization complements my roles.

Becoming organized for ministry includes having a desk that serves you. What does your desk look like? Is the top piled high with papers, envelopes, mail, articles, and/or uncompleted projects? If so, you need to consider organizing your desk to serve your needs. Uncluttered desks are more conducive to productive administrative work and creativity.

I became more aware of what a time-waster a cluttered desk can be when I visited a minister friend's office. We were discussing a recent conference mailing and were questioning something that had been said in the article. My friend said, "I have it right here. Let me check to see exactly what was said."

His desk had papers piled in every available space. I waited as he searched through several piles, mumbling, "I know it's here somewhere." After a few minutes, I left for my office where I knew exactly where to look for the correspondence. Incidentally, several days later he called me and asked if I had found my copy since his had "somehow mysteriously disappeared." It's probably still on his desk in one of those interesting piles which serve no practical use!

What is the alternative? The church professional's desk should include a file drawer for those files (calendar, committees) which are referred to regularly. The deep file drawer in my desk is my "active filing system" which includes my calendar/file. There is a file folder labeled for each month. In each folder is data concerning special observances, speaking engagements, bulletin resources, newsletter items, wedding information forms, and other materials pertaining to the month's activities. I always know where to go for information pertaining to a specific month and do not spend time looking through a pile of papers.

I also use a "four-box system" on a bookcase near my desk. The boxes are like those envelopes or standard typing paper come in. They are labeled IA (Immediate Action), P (Pending), RM (Reading Material), and F (File). (These terms suit my organizational system and style. You may want to develop more appropriate terms for your use.) With such a system, there is a place for materials awaiting processing.

My IA (Immediate Action) box contains those materials that require just that — immediate action. In this category are letters that need to be answered now, reports that have a deadline, and other projects which must be completed, based upon the priority of the task.

The box labeled P (Pending) contains materials which need to be processed within the next several weeks, correspondence awaiting a reply, and other materials which I need soon but which do not require immediate action.

RM (Reading Material) is a temporary storage place for articles to be read at another time. I receive numerous weekly magazines and parishioners often give me interesting articles. I scan the magazines and tear out articles which look interesting. These are placed in my RM box. Several times a week I retrieve two or three from the box and take them with me. It is always good to have these articles to read during unavoidable waiting periods. Articles that are worth keeping are filed in my more permanent "inactive filing system" according to topic and may later be retrieved as a resource for a sermon or program.

Every church professional should have his/her personal filing cabinet and system. File folders, and lots of them, should be standard issue. The filing cabinet should store resources and records which are not used daily, and is essential for storing more permanent records and information. My metal filing cabinet (which I refer to as my "inactive filing system" because it is used less frequently than my desk files) has four drawers and is quite adequate in size. This same file has served me for more than twenty years in ministry. The key to its use is to know what to put in it and when to clean it out so the system doesn't become overloaded or obsolete. For me, summer months or moving time are usually the most appropriate occasions for cleaning out my filing cabinet.

Let's consider a few other suggestions that time-management experts have found helpful. Clear your desk completely (or organize it by arranging papers neatly in piles, etc.) before leaving the office each day. This practice helps you get off to a good start the next day so you can begin immediately on the tasks for the day rather than using valuable time getting your work space ready for productive work. Another is to spend a few moments at the close of each day reviewing your next day's agenda. Are materials and resources readily available for the projects you plan? Do you know where they are? Why not collect them so they will be readily available?

Finally, develop and use a filing system which best serves your needs. The one described here works for me. The important thing is that you develop and use a system that works for you. Don't think that you are wasting time by taking a few minutes each day to get organized. Begin now to improve the organization of your resources. Using the check list (Exercise 7) which follows should provide the direction necessary to become better organized for ministry.

An Organizing-for-Ministry Check List

1. Organize desk. ☐

2. Look around office and eliminate clutter. ☐

3. Establish a twelve-month file folder system. ☐

4. Develop additional appropriate file systems. ☐

5. Clean out present files. ☐

6. Develop and use forms to assist in planning
   and record-keeping. ☐

7. List all administrative responsibilities
   and prioritize them. ☐

8. Review administrative tasks with
   governing body. ☐

9. Review library. Organize books according
   to categories; eliminate those which are
   no longer useful. ☐

10. Determine what is needed in office to
    make tasks more efficient. ☐

Exercise 7

Part II

Practical Helps for
More Effective Time Use

Chapter Six

Gaining Control of Your Time

Control of time is gained by examining ways we use it and then making adjustments to our life styles. Misused time is a result of well-established patterns of behavior. To change behavior we must learn why we do what we do, and then make modifications. This requires an active rather than a passive approach to time use. An active approach puts you in control of how and why you choose to use time as you do. A passive approach means that other people determine your priorities and demand time from you. Ask yourself these questions relating to your time use: 1. "Who (or what) controls how I use my time?" 2. "How can I gain more control over my time through behavior modification?"

An examination of your time logs should help you answer these questions. When reviewing your time logs, examine your behavior in view of the question, "Is this activity a legitimate function of my ministry?" Examine how you make decisions relating to time use. What areas demand the most of your time? What ways are you presently using time that are less than beneficial to your ministry?

Three practices are worth considering: *delegating, controlling settings* (meetings and appointments), and *controlling interruptions*.

It was Monday and the staff had gathered for a meeting. The pastor began by asking each staff member to report on projects in process, and to raise any issues and/or concerns.

The director of Christian education began: "Several of the youth leaders have suggested that it would be nice if we had a drink machine in the building."

"I thought we had agreed to get one," responded the choir director. "Wasn't someone going to look into getting one?"

"I remember we agreed that it was a good idea," said the secretary, "but I don't remember who was going to check on it. Was I supposed to do that?"

The pastor vaguely remembered that this subject had come up at a previous staff meeting. Ready to move on to other matters, he said, "I think we all agree it would be a good idea to have a drink machine. Now, would anyone like to check on the specific arrangements?"

There was silence. Finally, he said, "Then I'll check on it when I have time."

One of the most difficult tasks for church professionals is that of delegating responsibility to others. We have to work at the task of delegating, because if given a choice of doing the work ourselves or asking others to do the work, most of us will do it ourselves. Delegation of tasks for ministry is important because it provides opportunities for others to become involved. It is the responsibility of church professionals to delegate so that more can be done in ministry.

The church professional should not be spending time doing any task that could be done as well by a competent lay person. Ask this question: "What am I now doing that could be done just as well by someone else?" When you discover the answer, *delegate*!

Delegation involves practicing good communication skills. If a task is delegated to someone else, be sure that communication is adequate to interpret the request and to keep you informed. Feedback is vital in delegation (communication). When delegating, set time limits so that the person responsible will know what's expected by when.

In the illustration of the staff meeting, putting into

practice these suggestions would have resulted in the issue being addressed the first time it came up. Since it wasn't addressed, it would have been beneficial for the pastor to have said in response to the secretary's question, "No, you weren't asked to look into it, but it would be helpful if you would and give me a report at the next staff meeting." Better yet, the staff member working with the youth counselors should have asked one of them to gather appropriate data, and then information calling for a decision could be shared with the staff.

Setting time frames for meetings and appointments can also help you gain better control of your time. Church professionals spend many hours in settings which can become great time wasters unless times are set for beginning and ending. The importance of effective time use in meetings was addressed earlier (chapter 4). Church professionals can influence the time frame of meetings as well as affect agendas. Time allotments for individual appointments should also be set. Indicating how much time you have to give a setting usually encourages persons to use time wisely. Remember, if someone else is controlling how you use your time, you have lost control!

It is important to control interruptions. If you have a secretary, this may not be a serious problem. Simply indicate when you do not desire to be disturbed and why. For example, setting times for sermon preparation or other major projects that call for uninterrupted blocks of time is vital. When a secretary is aware of these times and circumstances, all phone calls (except emergencies) can be held and she or he can assist in educating the congregation concerning this priority. A secretary can also be a great help in screening unimportant calls and in providing information requested by the caller.

If you do not have a secretary, invest in a telephone

answering machine so that calls may be screened, received, and returned at times convenient to your schedule.

There are some things you can do to control walk-in interruptions. If you don't want to be disturbed, keep your office door closed. An open door is an invitation to "come in." Place an appropriate sign on your door: "In sermon preparation (or other activity): Available at _____ (time)." This will help interpret your work and the time given to it.

If someone persistent or who cannot be avoided interrupts you, be polite but, if he or she walks in, get up and remain standing. State your situation: "You've caught me at a bad time, as I'm up against a deadline. Can we get together later?" Then, suggest a time which fits your schedule. Most people will honor this request.

Of course, these suggestions apply to casual drop-ins, and do not apply to genuine emergencies. A (church) professional should be able to re-establish priorities at a moment's notice based upon vital emerging needs.

In summary, control over time is gained by modifying behavior so that **you** are in control. Delegation and control are important disciplines in the art of effective time use. Setting time limits for tasks also leads to more effective and productive use of time. Gaining control of your time is up to you. Don't forget: if you don't control your time, someone else will.

Chapter Seven

Planning and Prioritizing

It was Monday and the monthly ministers' meeting was about to begin. Buddy and Carol were enjoying the coffee fellowship preceding the meeting. George entered the room looking anxious and joined in the conversation.

"What's the matter, George?" Buddy asked. "You look like you had a rough weekend."

"No more than usual," George replied. "I just have so much to do this week I don't know where to begin. Know what I mean?"

"I know just what you mean," responded Carol. "I really don't have time to be here either. Maybe we'll get out early today. I have a thousand things to do."

"I'm not sure getting out early will help either of you," said Buddy. "You both are always busy and never seem to have enough time. Maybe you're trying to do too much. Perhaps you should ask yourselves, 'What is the most important thing I want to accomplish today?'"

Time-management consultants and business administrators suggest that the way a person spends the first fifteen minutes of the work day is crucial, for during that time the stage is set for how productive the day will be. Persons who have time-management problems are usually those who are trying to do too many things simultaneously and have no plan of action for what they hope to accomplish during the day. The basic strategy for using time effectively includes planning and prioritizing. You need a game plan for your work each day and each week. Otherwise your time will be used on whatever happens to cross your desk or with whomever demands it. Actions of others will shape your work and you will find yourself dealing with plans and priorities not your own.

The noted economist and management consultant Peter Drucker coined the term "management by objectives" more than thirty years ago. Such a concept involves thinking in terms of specifics rather than generalities. This concept is helpful in time management.

Begin by making a list of two or three things you hope to accomplish (objectives) in each given time period. Such objectives should meet what has been called the "SAM" test: they should be *specific, attainable, and measureable*. Setting objectives in your ministry (both short-range and long-range) provides self-motivation often lacking in ministry. Effective time users never wait to "get around to it." They have a "to do" list based on a plan of action, and they schedule appropriate time for the completion of each task.

For example, the importance of setting regular pastoral visitation objectives warrants an action plan. Weekly review of the church membership (and feedback on Sunday) will determine who needs pastoral attention. Intentionally setting aside specific times for visitation in hospitals, homes and institutions with specific goals (persons and needs) in mind will ensure that this aspect of ministry is accomplished. If visitation objectives are not established, fewer persons are seen. Intentionally setting aside specific nights weekly for visitation of new member prospects and/or members, and counseling, (and other regular responsibilities) will establish a more productive routine. If no plan of action exists to guide your appointment-making and other responsibilities, it becomes difficult to maintain a balance and some aspect of ministry will be neglected. Unless plans are made for various aspects of ministry, we are not as intentional as we should be in fulfilling these responsibilities.

Allocation of time for the completion of objectives results in more effective time use and gives the church professional a sense of accomplishment which is difficult to experience due to the nature of ministry. Studies prove that the more time spent in advance planning for a project, the less total time required to do it. Therefore, the most effective users of time begin by organizing each day according to a work plan of action determined according to objectives to be accomplished.

Time use is categorized according to the following: 1. urgent, 2. important, 3. necessary, 4. busy-work, 5. nonproductive or a waste of time. Those persons who make the most of time have learned to separate important things from the trivial.

After you have outlined work to be done (plan by objectives), do the most important ones first (prioritize)!

Prioritizing includes determining how important the work is, when it needs to be accomplished, and setting a time frame or deadline to complete the task. Until a deadline is set for a project, it will not become a priority, for we only give time to what we (or someone else) consider(s) to be important.

There are many ways to establish priorities. In some cases, built-in deadlines establish priorities. For example, every pastor identifies with the Sunday morning deadline for having a completed sermon for the worship service. Knowing when a task must be completed helps determine the priority the task is given. If the task does not have an established deadline, set one so that the work becomes a part of scheduled activities.

In prioritizing various tasks of ministry, a numbering system can be helpful. Assign tasks numbers: 1, if *urgent*, 2, if *important*, and 3, if *necessary*. Obviously all the "ones" get attention first and tasks are upgraded from three to one based upon deadlines set for completion of each. Using days of the week is also an effective way of prioritizing task for ministry. Placing the appropriate initial for each day next to the task on a "to do this week" list is an effective method. A system of prioritizing that works for you must be developed and utilized to determine the order in which objectives are completed.

In addition to daily and weekly planning, practice long-range planning by objectives. What would you like to accomplish six months from now, both professionally and personally? Setting objectives and prioritizing leads to greater productivity in ministry, and time-management practitioners live more productive lives!

Chapter Eight

Dealing with Time-Robbers

Time-management experts claim the average person wastes two or three hours each day. When we examine how we spend time, most of us can identify a number of "time-robbers." A "time-robber" is something which keeps us from doing things which have more value or importance. Time-robbers are unproductive, low-value activities. They may be external (caused by people or events) or internal (the result of personal choices). More effective time-use results from identifying and eliminating or controlling as many time-wasting activities as possible.

To identify external time-robbers, keep an interruption log for several days. Include the type of interruption, time of occurrence, amount of time spent, who initiated the interruption, and the nature of business transacted. Examine the log against the question, "Were these interruptions a vital part of my work?" If the answer is "no," then ask this question: "What can I do to avoid future interruptions of this nature?"

Examination of your time logs will help you discover some internal time-robbers. As you identify behavior which leads to wasted time, you will also need to ask, "Why do I spend my time this way?" Many time-robbers are a result of poor habits calling for behavior modification. Not all time-robbers can be eliminated, but identifying those over which you do have control enables you to make decisions leading to more effective and productive time use.

Participants in time-management workshops identify a number of activities and events as time-robbers. At the top of the list are interruptions from telephone calls, drop-in visitors, and procrastination. Let's look at these primary time-robbers and see how they can be better controlled.

The telephone caller requested to speak to the pastor and the secretary put the call through.

"Reverend, can you tell me when the fellowship supper is scheduled?" asked the caller.

The pastor, interrupted from writing, reached for the church calendar and discovered that several fellowship meals were planned for the month.

"There are several scheduled," he responded. "We have our monthly family night and several circles are planning a meal. Which one are you interested in?"

"Oh, I meant the Fellowship Circle's dinner. I can't remember if it's this week or next."

Having provided the answer, the pastor found it difficult to return to the article he was writing. He wished someone else had handled the call so the interruption could have been avoided.

The whole transaction took three minutes. Multiplied by a number of similar calls in any given day, a pastor will spend a considerable amount of time in unnecessary activities.

Telephone interruptions lead to inefficiency in work. When you do not desire to be disturbed, take action so that incoming calls will not become interruptions. Secretaries can play a vital role by screening calls. In an analysis of my telephone interruptions log, I discovered that the majority of my calls were information related and could be handled by my secretary (or someone else who has knowledge of the church calendar and activities). I requested my secretary to offer assistance to the caller before referring the caller to me. A simple, "May I help you?" is usually sufficient to determine the nature of the call and who can best handle it. If they do get through, refer information-related callers back to the secretary or other appropriate staff member. This establishes an information flow pattern and trains repeat callers to use it instead of you.

Answering machines are helpful tools for screening calls and should be in every church office where there is no secretary. Otherwise the church professional will spend most of his or her time responding to incoming calls. If you do have to answer a phone call at an inopportune time, be in control of the conversation and move as rapidly as possible toward termination.

Every office has drop-in visitors. They may be co-workers who just stop to chat, someone with a question, or with something serious on his or her mind. The church professional should be ready to deal with genuine requests for help and reestablish priorities for time use based on emerging needs. Persons with legitimate concerns are not time-robbers. The "time-robber" is the casual drop-in who "just stops by" and who has no legitimate claim over time allotted to another priority. It is not rude to inform persons when it is not convenient to be interrupted. Chapter 6 suggests specific ways to control walk-in interruptions.

Procrastination is another time-robber. Procrastination is avoidance or postponement of an activity in favor of some other (more favorable) activity. A number of reasons have been identified as to why people procrastinate:

- the unpleasantness of a given task
- a feeling of inadequacy
- lack of understanding
- lack of commitment
- fear of failure
- fear of success
- the feeling that the task is overwhelming
- fatigue
- stress

We tend to procrastinate when tasks are unpleasant, difficult or overwhelming. Postponement of unpleasant tasks is an attempt to make things easier. However, such action (or lack of action) increases the unpleasantness and creates anxiety.

Procrastination can be controlled by identifying its reason. The next time you find yourself procrastinating, review the reasons included here and identify the cause. Then you can find a solution.

The best way to handle the temptation to procrastinate over certain tasks is to do them first. Some procrastination can be overcome by using "prime time" (when you are fresh and at your best) for unpleasant tasks. When tasks are large and tend to be overwhelming, they should be broken into smaller, more workable tasks. Set deadlines and give yourself rewards for completion. Make use of meditation. Find ways to relieve stress. These are some of the ways procrastination can be conquered.

Other notorious "time-robbers" include:

- failure to delegate
- inefficiency
- poor planning
- non-productive meetings
- poor communication
- lack of priorities
- disorganization
- the inability to say no

You can add to this list. The important thing is to identify *your* time-robbers and find solutions. Most solutions are common sense once the problem has been identified.

You can identify time-robbers by asking of all your activities: "What would happen if this were not done at all?" If the answer is "nothing would happen," then the activity represents a time-robber and you should stop doing it. Identifying your time-robbers and solutions will lead to better control over your time and will free up valuable time for more productive pursuits.

Chapter Nine

Time-saving
Practices and Techniques

The heart of any time-management system is a calendar notebook which serves a variety of functions. The most effective system includes an appointment calendar, record keeper, and a workbook. Using one calendar notebook for recording all professional activities helps coordinate one's professional and personal life. I have found a three-ring notebook style calendar to be most beneficial. The calendar provides space for daily appointments, and the notebook provides space for recording business expenses (mileage, meals, and miscellaneous items), a "Things To Do" form and weekly and monthly summary record forms. There is also a place for frequently called phone numbers, and blank sheets for note taking. Examination of the many appointment calendars on the market today provides assistance in developing a management tool that suits your needs.

Working hours can be more productive by identifying the time(s) during the day when you are at your best. Some do their most creative and productive work in the mornings. Others function better in the afternoon or evening. Undertaking any task requiring you to be at your best at a time other than your most productive "prime time" leads to inferior work or procrastination. It is important to discover when you function best for various tasks. Then schedule tasks according to the type of work and the energy level required. Use your best hours of the day for the most important (or difficult) tasks. You "save time" when you use time to the best advantage.

"Travel time" can also be used productively. Many

church professionals spend an average of two hours a day in an automobile. For example, morning commute time can be used productively by reviewing the day's agenda. This prepares you for the day's activities and valuable time isn't spent in deciding what needs to be done first on arrival at the office. Jotting down names of persons who need to be contacted, or noting activities that need to be addressed during the day will help give direction to the day's agenda. Mentally reflecting over the day's goals gets the day off to a good start. Listening to educational tapes is a good alternative to listening to the radio, especially on trips. Making the best use of travel time means using available resources and technology to make time use more productive.

Keeping a "to do" list is a helpful time-saving technique. There are many ways this can be done. Some professionals carry 3x5 cards at all times. The cards contain notes of things to do and are readily available to add new tasks as they arise. They can easily be organized according to priority. Others make daily or weekly "to do" lists, with priorities. Items are checked off upon completion. This is the method that works for me. I use a "To Do This Week" form to list all activities and contacts for each week. These forms provide records of tasks undertaken and accomplished in given time frames and encourage long-range planning.

Many church professionals spend considerable time making pastoral visits. When planning home visits, phoning ahead to make an appointment will insure that your trip will not be wasted. In anticipation of the actual visit, plan your agenda. Determine the purpose of your visit in advance and when you arrive, move the conversation toward the fulfilment of that purpose. Keep in mind that in some cases adequate contacts with parishioners can be made over the telephone.

Bill was grocery shopping when a parishioner spotted him. "Reverend," the parishioner began, "I am so glad that I ran in to you. I've been meaning to call you all week to ask you to speak at my Circle meeting. We would love to have you. We meet on the second Tuesday of the month. You can come, can't you?"

Without thinking, Bill reached for his pocket calendar, opened it to the date and saw that it was open.

"It looks clear," he said. "I guess I can make it. Let me know what you want me to talk about."

Later when Bill was informed of the subject to be addressed, he discovered that it would take considerable time to prepare an appropriate talk. He realized that he had over-committed himself. In addition to the extra hours of preparation required, it meant another week without a night home with his family.

"If only I had said 'no,' " he thought. But it was too late.

Of all the time-saving techniques ever developed, the most effective of all is the frequent use of the word "no." It is rather ironic that one of the first words learned as children is one of the most difficult to say as adults. The inability to say "no" is especially a problem for church professionals. Many times the response "yes" is given without thinking through the decision concerning the amount of time the commitment represents. It is helpful never to say "yes" on the spot. A more appropriate response is, "I'll be happy to consider it and let you know after I consult my appointment book." This response allows time to think through what is being requested, to consider how much time is involved, and whether saying "yes" will be a burden upon an already-overworked schedule. Every commitment affects one's personal, social and family life. It is easy to fill up the appointment book with meetings and appointments. The church professional must constantly guard against over-commitment. Saying "no" is the most effective practice toward that goal.

Now is the time to begin to put the following time-saving principles and techniques into practice:

- Establish measureable goals, and then plan accordingly (develop a game plan to achieve your goal(s).
- Learn to prioritize and do the most important things first.
- Set deadlines and reward yourself upon completion.
- Organize your desk/office to serve you.
- Have a place for everything and keep everything in its place.
- Develop a workable file system.
- Handle papers only once (discard, process and/or file).
- Use forms and files for storage of data.
- Use one calendar for commitments.
- Maintain a daily activities log of business and travel expenses.
- Learn to say "no."
- Master your appointment calendar.
- Schedule flexibility into your daily agenda.
- Schedule personal as well as professional time.
- Make time for yourself, including regular days off.
- Use "prime time" for most difficult tasks.
- Open your mail over a trash can.
- Practice grouping of work projects.
- Use waiting and travel time productively.
- Practice ETA (estimated time for accomplishment).
- Spend a few moments in "night-before" planning.
- Clear your desk (or organize it) before leaving the office.
- Carry a pen and note pad (or 3x5 cards).
- Identify and eliminate time-wasters.
- Know yourself, your strengths and your limitations.

- Separate the important from the trivial.
- Learn to delegate.
- Use available technology — computer, recorders (cassette and video), telephone, copy and answering machines.
- Keep periodic time logs to insure that you use your time wisely.

Utilizing time-management principles and techniques will result in more productive work. Church professionals who don't manage time effectively often experience frustration, stress, and burn-out. That's why the practice of good time-management principles is so important.

Chapter Ten

Taking Time to be Holy

Taking time to become holy (growing in relationship with God) is essential if we are to be good stewards of our greatest God-given resource, *the gift of time*. The call to every Christian is a call to holiness. Holiness has to do with the degree to which one becomes consecrated or committed to God's will and purposes for life. Holiness does not come automatically in the life of Christians, but results from the practice of a number of disciplines in the process of becoming what God wants us to be.

Time has meaning and purpose when viewed as a gift to be used. The most important time in the life of a church professional, therefore, is that time with the Time-Giver. In response to the recognition that all time is from God, church professionals need to understand the meaning of time in relationship to the Time-Giver, take time to focus on the purpose(s) of ministry to which God calls them, and discover the strengths and resources which equip them to do ministry.

Time can be defined in several ways. The well-known concept of time is "chronos," a unit of measure such as clock time or a day on the calendar. Events are measured as they occur at specific times according to the clock or the day of the week. Such time is evenly distributed and predictable. "Chronos" signifies time as an interval, a period, a quantity.

To that understanding of time the Christian faith adds another dimension: "kairos" time. "Kairos" is defined as "the right time" or those "special times." It is the time referred to by the writer of Ecclesiastes when he wrote, "To everything there is a season, and a time for everything under the heaven." (Ecclesiastes 3:1) In "kairos" time all events are viewed according to God's understanding of time, which is measured primarily by events of *quality*, rather than *quantity*.

For example, "chronos" can be understood as a date on a calendar, whereas "kairos" is a season characterized by events. When time is viewed predominately as "chronos," one tends to see it as abstract and as having little meaning. When viewed as "kairos," time is seen as given by God, meaningful and purposeful, and every moment has the potential of some significant happening. "Chronos" is time to be controlled, managed or used; "kairos" is time to be understood as God-given and responded to in order to serve God's purpose(s) in time.

The key to meaningful time use is how to control "chronos" so that we can experience "kairos." This understanding of time in relationship to the Time-Giver is essential in the development of a theological doctrine of time use.

We begin to focus on the purpose of ministry to which we are called by asking, "What is God calling me to do as an agent charged with the responsibility of assisting in Kingdom building?" "What do I understand to be the primary ministry to which God is calling me?" These questions must continually be asked by the church professional who, in turn, must raise these questions with church members and leaders. Together the church professional and church members should seek answers to such questions in order to find direction for ministry.

There are three spiritual disciplines which will strengthen persons for the tasks of ministry: *prayer, study,* and *meditation.* Church professionals should perfect a pattern of time use undergirded by time spent in these meaningful disciplines leading to holiness. The purpose here is not to provide specific resources for improving devotional or prayer life (there are many materials already available to assist you with this), but to suggest ways to improve your time use leading to spiritual growth toward holiness.

1. Prayer is vital in the process of becoming holy because it involves communicating with the Holy. It is interesting to note that of all the things Jesus taught his disciples, the only thing they ever asked of him was to teach them to pray. (See Luke 11:1-4.) Scriptures provide us with many examples of the priority of prayer in Jesus' life. He withdrew often from the tasks of his ministry to find renewal through prayer. (See Mark 1:35.)

Jesus found those quiet places for communication and meditation with his Heavenly Father. These times of prayer provided confirmation for the direction of his ministry and strengthened him for the tasks he faced. He came away from those quiet times of prayer and meditation renewed and strengthened to continue his mission. If prayer is communication with God, then it is important to keep the channels of communication open through regular contact. We need to say with the disciples, "Lord, teach us to pray," and then listen for his guidance so that our ministry might be according to God's will and purposes for our lives.

2. Church professionals should practice the discipline of *studying the Scriptures*. Answers are available for direction in ministry when we utilize the channels of communication available through prayer *and* Bible study. As we study the Scriptures, we come to a deeper understanding of the church's nature and the mission to which the church is being called in our day. Studying Scripture enables us to find answers to life's crucial questions. Church professionals need to model for

others the importance of the discipline of study so that they, too, might grow in the faith and understanding of God's purpose(s) for life.

3. Taking time to become holy also includes time for *personal meditation*. Meditation involves setting a quiet time apart for reflective listening with expectation. Often when God's spokespersons had a word of importance to proclaim to the people of their day, they prefaced their remarks with the imperative, "Listen!" God continues to speak in various ways today but we need to listen for the message. It is important to find a place conducive to meaningful meditation. What are the possible places for you to go to find that quiet time for meditation and solitude?

The most conducive place of meditation for me is the sanctuary of my church at times during the week when no one else is around. Time spent in silence is valuable. Sometimes the needs of my congregation come more clearly into focus; a member comes to mind whom I need to contact out of pastoral concern, or in those brief moments, I am led to offer a special prayer. Other times an idea for a sermon is born. Such experiences involve reflective listening for God's word for life. There are times when we need to "be still," and listen for God's message.

Specifically-planned experiences are also valuable for spiritual growth. Participation in events such as spiritual life retreats provides such opportunities. Times spent in intentional spiritual growth away from daily responsibilities refresh us for continuing ministry.

Participation in regular support groups for growth, study and fellowship are helpful and productive. I have been involved in a ministers' support group for the past four years. It meets each Wednesday morning at eight o'clock. Gathering at that hour represents quite a discipline for us, but we respond faithfully to the covenant of mutual support and commitment to spiritual growth. This time is given a priority in our schedules because the experience provides refreshment and renewal. It is a time for becoming "holy" and "wholistic" as we share our lives and ministry with each other.

Church professionals must take time to practice regular disciplines which lead to spiritual growth and faith development. The practice of spiritual disciplines which lead to holiness prepares us for the demands and requirements of faithful ministry. Through such experiences our spirits are renewed and we find inner strength to respond to the challenges of a demanding profession. As church professionals, we need to keep ever before us the example of the Master Teacher whose life leads us to holiness and wholeness.

A Prayer Concerning Time

Lord God, help us to remember that time is your gift to us. You have taught us that "to everything there is a season and a time for everything under heaven." We thank you for every moment of every day. Help us make the most of the time you give us. Grant us the wisdom to use time wisely as faithful stewards. Strengthen and renew us so that we might be equipped for the ministry to which you have called us. Lord, take all that we are as servants and enable us to grow into holiness. So may we, in time, come to know all the joys of the faith. Amen

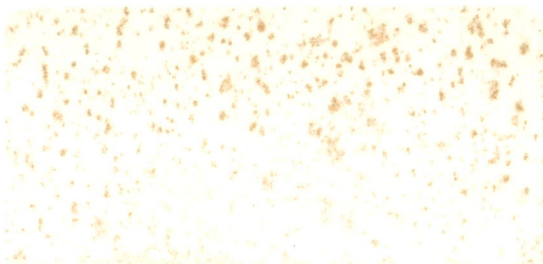

Take Time . . .

Take time to work, for work gives life a sense of purpose and contributes to the good of society.

Take time to think, for in thinking the mind is used creatively.

Take time to laugh and play, for these give life pleasure and break down barriers.

Take time to dream, for dreams help shape the hopes and possibilities of tomorrow.

Take time to love, for loving gives life ultimate worth and fulfilment.

Take time to relax, for relaxing gives the body time for refreshment and renewal.

Take time to read, for reading enriches the mind and restores the soul.

Take time to worship, for in worshiping the Giver of time we are inspired to be faithful stewards of each God-given moment.

GENERAL THEOLOGICAL SEMINARY
NEW YORK

DATE DUE

NOV 28 89		
NOV 30 '90		
DEC 26 '90		

About the Author

R. Franklin Gillis, Jr., is an ordained minister and member of the Virginia Conference of the United Methodist Church. Dr. Gillis' ministry has been varied. In addition to pastoral appointments he has served as Youth Minister, Director of Wesley Foundation Campus Ministry, and District Program Coordinator. He presently serves as the senior pastor of the historic Monumental United Methodist Church in Portsmouth, Virginia.

A native of Hampton, Virginia, Gillis is a graduate of Randolph-Macon College (BA), Wesley Theological Seminary (M.Div.) and Lancaster Theological Seminary (D.Min.).

Dr. Gillis is an active person who enjoys life and seeks to make the most of each day. In addition to his pastoral responsibilities, he is the President of the Virginia United Methodist Communications, Inc. and serves on a number of Conference Committees. He designs and leads various retreats and workshops for church professionals and church leaders. In addition to time-management workshops, Gillis also leads stress management, church planning, preaching and communication seminars. His special interests include video, photography, and travel.